# THE SACRED
# HEART MOTEL

# THE SACRED HEART MOTEL

*Poems*

## Grace Kwan

**METONYMY PRESS**

Montreal, Quebec

The Sacred Heart Motel
ISBN 978-1-998898-16-9 (paperback)
ISBN 978-1-998898-17-6 (EPUB)
ISBN 978-1-998898-18-3 (PDF)

Metonymy Press
PO Box 143 Succ Saint-Dominique
Montreal QC H2S 3K6 CANADA

Printed and bound in Canada by Imprimerie Gauvin
First edition, first printing

Cover art and design by Niki Hoi
Edited by Eli Tareq El Bechelany-Lynch
Copy edited by Sophie Dufresne and Oliver Fugler
Interior design by Ashley Fortier

Some of the pieces in this collection were previously published. Please see the notes and acknowledgements on page 81.

Thank you to A.R. Clegg for their generous donation in memory of their brother, Graham Clegg.

We acknowledge the support of the Canada Council for the Arts. Nous remercions le Conseil des arts du Canada de son soutien.

 Canada Council    Conseil des arts
for the Arts      du Canada

Library and Archives Canada Cataloguing in Publication

Title: The Sacred Heart Motel : poems / Grace Kwan.
Names: Kwan, Grace, author.
Identifiers: Canadiana (print) 20240470818 | Canadiana (ebook) 20240470931 | ISBN 9781998898169
   (softcover) | ISBN 9781998898183 (PDF) | ISBN 9781998898176 (EPUB)
Subjects: LCGFT: Poetry.
Classification: LCC PS8621.W34 S23 2024 | DDC C811/.6—dc23

Dépôt légal, Bibliothèque et Archives nationales du Québec, 2024.

MIX
Paper
FSC
www.fsc.org    FSC® C100212

*For migrants & visitors. To A.*

*The shape of a life can feel like a past tense; something we sense only after it has been acquired.*

– Sara Ahmed

# *Directory*

## THE MOONLIGHT SUITE,

*originally furnished in 1970. View*
*of stone-dug pond, firefly brim.*

*Queen mattress, spacious kitchenette, loveseat*

*from which to watch the news.*
*Privacy and sanctuary for the entire stay.*

*Every June, the TV plays only a loop*
*from a nature documentary. Wolves' silhouette mouths*

*tipped at a boneshard moon, overlaid with Satie's*
*Gnossienne No. 5, as if singing*

*to the night or maybe eating it whole.*
*Management will inform summer guests*

*prior to booking and will not be held liable or offer any refund.*

# BALLET FLATS

My first designer shoes delivered,
vintage, at twenty-four. Leather uppers
and silver hardware to punctuate satin ribbons.
Barefoot, waiting, I danced balancés
on the bathmat. Sweeping arms, curved to hold.
The mall was demolished nine years ago,
so I self-mythologize with Prabal and Proenza.
You danced on frosted steps once,
ready to bus to the grocery store
with an eight-year-old on your heels. Snow
soaked through your shoes. Ex-dancer, thirty-seven
in The Bay where the beds were clouds
and I wanted to buy rubber rain boots.
The mall smelled of popcorn and pretzels
when we walked out of the store, hungry.

# EVENING GOWNS

of chiffon and taffeta, cheekbones
dipped in diamond dust,
a self who laughed into
a man's shoulder. Face
tilted to smile at his
lips before kissing them,
leaving a rust-red imprint.
Studied that imprint;
if she looked at me
like that, would she look
past every earnest groove or find it
rather nice to look at just because,
just because. Stalk the shadows
of a rose garden, eyes dimmed
by the drink in her hand.
Ballroom music, poisoned chalice.
Smile at my lips before
kissing them.
The red darkens on his
mouth, blurs
and all slips away into
the void of the man:
the roses, the party,
even me.

# GLUE TRAP

My heart looks like the old yellow house where thin, mouse-bitten
walls separated our part of the basement from another
Chinese family. We could hear their daughter practice tongue
twisters, they could hear my mother scream when I went too far
in my careless teenage obstinacy. She came home one day
with a pink plastic bag of glue traps for the mice who tormented
the strings in my piano and chewed holes in their rice sacks.
I could hear it chirp, the first one caught in the entrance hall
between our two chambers, as the adults circled it.
My mother slipped back inside after convening with the other
parents, told me the father would get rid of it. Squeaks crescendoed
when the sheet of glue started to travel—the father lifting it,
hands close enough for the mouse to smell sulphur, walking it
outside where, beneath a smoky moon, I heard him
bring down the hammerhead. Or rather, I couldn't hear
any more chittering. I rewound and tried to count the heartbeats
between squeak and silence, the jammy crush of fur and
skull. I've been having these moments more
and more: time feels like a rotten tooth, and my body sinks
into its wormy cavity. I've hauled myself through
this life on delusion alone, sidestepping puddles
while I wore rain boots. Taught myself how to love from
imitation. And I can't deny every time someone tells, confesses,

intimates that they love me, I feel a deep grief ripple
out from inside me—the dearths left by mice
with broken heads and songs unfinished.

# I. LOVE

At morning's volta, each dewdrop
Gathered at the knife tip of grass before dropping

Drinks enough magic to become. Bead of
Starlight to be sewn, seed which will grow once dropped,

Or a mirror insisting your face—not mine
Nor my lover's illusory swan-drop.

Fingers slide up the grass and catch
Your perfect sphere for it to slip and drop

Into each morning's recapitulation,
The foamfroth break before eventide drops

Its melodic carcass. When time came for Sirius,
you followed as his eyelids dropped.

# EXODUS

Body is what we call
ourselves, Christ as the head,

Men fancying themselves eyelash,
tongue-bud, temple, teeth,

Aaron most of all,
booming with devotion

from the throat
of the congregation.

I know the existence
of Aaron's nameless son

only in frisson of darkened
marrow and plasma.

I'm preoccupied with infection,
torn stitches, scars

and scabbing ... but most
often, I linger on

phantom pain, the seeping
ache come twilight as if

that pinioned appendage still fled,
trying to tell the rest

of the body which knits itself violet
that it still is—and never stopped—

# CLOVER

Your mother has, I'm sure, told
you about the rabbit on the moon?
Mine tells of the wild hare born
to a pair of pet rabbits in a house
down the trail

—or sometimes monkeys, sometimes otters,
sometimes a toad, but mostly rabbits.
Downy grey things with dumpling bums
and periscope ears.

In any case, the hare ate no pellets,
only mouthfuls of clover staining his
maw yellow, jumped too high
with muscles that knew the wind
like an old friend and finally one evening leapt

and landed on the moon. He sleeps
as the moon turns to shadow,
refusing cold starlight
and eternity's gaze, but
every month, when his perch swivels,
allowing him a view of brushstroke clouds,

water churning slow as azure tree sap,
he sticks his paws in those craters and makes
himself useful. Grinds bitter powder
for the sick, sticky rice cakes
for the hungry,
all the while noticing—

he's never noticed before,
between monolith ice caps—

islands green as clover springing up
                    as if underfoot
as if he can almost taste bent grass
rising to the sun while his shadow flees
the scene.

## KITCHEN: BACK EXIT

A row of hairnets, jumpsuits, aprons, blazers,
seen sitting on empty crates with legs crossed,

unaware of one another.

                                          Each gazes
to a pinhole horizon off to the side.
Someone has erected a makeshift scarecrow on the
balcony of an apartment far

across the alleyscape—mannequin shaped like
half a child with bottle-blond hair.

                                      Workweek schedule
pinned by the kitchen door under a list of 86s.
A flint wheel spits up an orange spark which recognizes
itself in the lighter's

gold casing. The mannequin shivers, then

                                          rocks forward.

# IN ONE DREAM I DIVE

forward into milky waves
a red twist of striated muscle
knifing into white
disappearing into purity
under a low-burning
primordial sky

## II. HONOUR

I first saw it

    In a scrim of stars
    Only visible in

The precise moment a
Lover turns over

    In bed, spilling
    Dreams from his ear. God of conquest,

Beholding the
Silhouette I saw
    Blood run, wisteria,

A planet drinking its
Fill, and I still remember

The song beneath the grass,
Clouds blindfolding stars,
    Leading even these hills to pledge

Themselves pink while I watch

    That shadow you tore into

    The horizon.

# NOTCH

*Saturn's rings are thought to be pieces of comets, asteroids, or shattered moons that broke up before they reached the planet, torn apart by Saturn's powerful gravity. They are made of billions of small chunks of ice and rock coated with other materials such as dust.*

*— NASA*

I string     This
is what I see when I
dream
        Tin can solar system
lined up in a father's eye     Sun

I bow to weightlessness

        that fills and levies
upon from outside

the body     I notch

I feather nylon
I clamp my teeth to

this pole     I pupil

I carbon head      I
broad steel rend      I waver

to the wind to cleave it
          wide open


          I splinter
bloom      I arrhythmia

# GENDER STUDIES

I light a lamp for the late nights to
pore over translations while others

hike through grey snow to reach parties;
sit with you and though I want to

am unable to look directly
for the halogen light swinging

untouched above your head.
Brush you with my hair;

listen; read because
beauty was once a country

I belonged to now I'm a migrant
placeless and still hovering

on the limn trying on wages
radium and high heels as a second language

debossed in cracked leather
bleeding like citizens onto onion skin.

A fly lands on your blue shoulder;
sirens sound and scatter the dorms.

# LUCKY STRIKE

You drive, blue.
Rain fractures in dim storefront halos.
The wipers groan and rattle.
Clouds parted just right, glitter of a city
high on a mountain at the end of the distant road,
man-made constellation on a thumbprint smudge.
Focus. A figure on the sidewalk with a dog.
Smoking. Smells like your father's menthol cigarettes.
He steps back to loosen the leash. Keeps stepping.
Keeps backing. You can't stop the car.
Off the curb, onto the road. Smoke
from his cigarette inhales itself back into
the gathering clump of ash. He passes through the car
or the car passes through him and he backpedals
all the way north to the city in the sky.
In the rearview the dog barks on the sidewalk.
Leash trailing up in the air, abandoned by gravity.

## NEXT DOOR, A BAR

*Police ruled it suspicious, the flame*
*which doused a forest, quiet*
*and greedy in its mythology.*

*A philosophical cohort came to settle*
*the matter having fumbled*
*their booking at the Fairmont.*

*Shared bedrooms in twos*
*and told us about their lives*
*through thin walls.*

*A half-dozen men*
*rationalized their way to*
*the bar shoulder to shoulder*
*with field notes and scuffed loafers.*

*When the speaker woke,*
*the noise it made was penned*
*as a lonely green wind.*

# HEAT WAVE

        Lavender stalks burble
from the back of your throat
the morning you wake

to the rabbit's water bowl
her long ears slack and tongue
floating like ripped silk

        silly to think of something
like summer's yolk breaking over fields
of flowers as anything but happenstance

this inability to spectate
this refusal of fortune crying

like an eldest daughter look
at all this disaster aren't you
lucky this lives

in your head and not your world
        where glaciers melt like
the ice cube you placed in her bowl

during the heat of night
                    purple rice calyxes lodging
in your windpipe you imitate the rhythm of baby's

breath the way you breathed in synchrony
with the rabbit
                    to assure yourself of her
life inside you the bouquet

exploding from Chekhov's gun
depending on the way it's pointed

a regret or an observation or
a kindness owed
                    and if you step out

inhale mown grass unleash it
on the back of your tongue you'll think
                    you know why the rabbit
lunges to snatch the dandelion

leaves from your hand

# PATHS

*after Joan Didion*

Sometimes I forget I love someone
and sometimes I scroll three years back on a childhood
friend's memory trying to learn her
sister's face trying to remember
why she disliked me in the end
and sometimes I see a hole in the shape of me
torn into the fabric of my life, widening
until it's no longer legible. If I leave this city,
crawl into a new shelf, the world
outside could be fire, could be pearl. Could be a love
letter, could be a body that needs my hands
or my words. But I wouldn't
know it.

# RATIONALE

Years ago, my mother
halved an avocado,
the knife interrupting
green butter so easily
it missed the pit and sliced her
finger, its brusque nerve.

Still she praises
my level head,
rational instructions—
apply pressure as you
drive yourself to the ER—
the avocado pit a planet
spinning slowly in its
red silk belt, a ruby
under certain compliments,

a tongue atrophied.
Why not love something that speaks
its beauty all the time, without
being asked? Without needing
to be earned? Why wait

for a life of colour from a
written word? Or does
writing it diffract control

somehow? Give back,
one autonomous morpheme
at a time,

the self
I never wanted?

# IN A SINCE-DEMOLISHED POOL

a row of steel heads spouted women, the Neptunian
roil of their dimpled skin.

Someone once dove
from the highest board and splattered

onto tile, red envelope of the body slit open.
I watched friends take the same spill

with trepidation, others with no hesitation
while a few stood huddled at the tip of the green tongue

for minutes before turning back, afraid.
Friendship moves different underwater,

like time. We'd submerge ourselves and scream
till our lungs bloomed apart at the seams and

when we resurfaced, nothing marked the passage
but our breath. We couldn't hear each other scream

underwater, only the small distant roar of our own
screams. We'd shower between naked women and towel off

and in winter puffers and scarves walk outside
to a playground and pussy willows.

When I lie down at the end of the night and
let go the cold of quaking muscle,

the love that I've been holding,
it comes out a gusty blue sigh.

# WHEN BILLIE HOLIDAY SANG

*I'm gonna love you like*
*nobody's loved you*
with the rain flickering
against my parted window
and sheets pooled
around my hips was when
I first felt the bottom
of my stomach suggest
it was perhaps less
the bottom than
the precipice and
my first thought was
to reach for your wrist.
A moonlit river was once
an inaccessible romance
vignetted by searchlights
chased by people
I didn't understand
with no hope of
participating in desire
until Billie sang
that note.
What is it about her

voice that cleaves
an octave's destiny
like the moon's unfolding
bolt over the sea?
I try to understand
how you love
music without interrogation
just the experience
of living from note to note
each breath lasting only as long
as it sustains the next.

## ART SHOW

String of baroque pearls
mercury-pink cuffing wrists in place
red lingerie a spool of thread on thimble hips
oakwood chair tepid sunlight polaroid flash
expired lipstick bullet crushed against mirror
lens refusing to take & light-blacked frame
recessed lights scattered onto photographs
colleagues pore over wine in hand before they leave
for steak frites at the eatery two blocks over
leaving you to contemplate the artwork a slim thigh
here curve of breast there body stuck on repeat
& ritenuto

## ROOM 209

features a double bed,
a standing shower,
and a vandalized Bible in the desk drawer.
No different from any other room,
but the staff know about
authors who penned broken-toothed
manuscripts here; years-long affairs
that left change for the magpies—
caps from cologne bottles, credit cards,
one leftover diamond earring
lodged in the shower drain.
And naturally—what's a love
story without its ghosts—
more than a few bullet
wounds in the floor. Groaning
like a tape recorder. Panting
like a heartbeat. The green
wallpaper anxiously lingers.

# IN ANOTHER DREAM

i spilled into a dimming
blue afternoon
on a raked stage
where rain fell from rafters
as taxis drove in and
out of the wings
and out-of-towners surfaced
from the glass of a hotel's door
to sink into taxis without
pause or parapluie
the orchestra pit slowly filling
with water while it rolled offstage
and rose to shoulders of cellists
their hair wet against their velvets

# INTERMISSION

Double bass reclined
sidelong in the spotlight
neck bared—
steel tendons belie tender rust. Whose
fingers are so lucky as to smell
of oxidized metal tonight? Light glimmers
off a maple shoulder but before I can think
*it begs for a kiss* she hauls herself upright
moseys offstage and I follow. Into the wings
arms of spruce whispering against me
hardwood sinking to loam underfoot then
sand. Looking around I shout
her name but the sea air snatches it
from my mouth gives it
to the tide and I haven't finished
speaking I want to be worth her
manipulation I walk with my body bent
against wind even though there is none, then I see the shape
and colour of her
approaching along blue shoreline
feet submerged in overturned sand face tilted
towards mine hand staying imaginary wind
from blowing the sweater off

that shoulder and my
relief aches a symphony.
The first violin draws breath.
The buffeting wind sounds
like a wrung A-string.

## III. TIME

Not the splice
    In the sun
        I once would've thought

But the hammock
    Between your heartbeats
        In the dusk

Teaching me patience
    Akin to the way
        The lightning bug lover

Releasing his catch
    In the reeds teaches me
        To love you

# THE SCORE

Thought today was gorgeous
enough to step out.
Two in the tennis court

hitting a ball back and forth.
Perfect weather to visualize violence

upon oneself. To think of the self as gorgeous,

and in these visions skin feels like the vesicle under the rind,
just-healed and bursting onto someone's tongue.

"Gorgeous," possibly the highest praise
anything can be given, also the starting point
from which all the praise blooms.

Tennis instructor said to aim the ball
so the opposition makes an unforced error.

I couldn't help it, again and again

I volleyed it towards the other's racket
begging, calling

open-mouthed

for the splay of sweet fruit.

# MY YEAR OF REST & EXPATRIATION

I'm having lunch with a girl
in an eatery playing Phoebe Bridgers;
funny how we aim at politics first thing
after a breakup. I tell her I do
hate her mom but really I miss
having a mother to do my grieving
for me. The most gorgeous things
people have made are always the things
they've made for themselves. I curate and curate
until the words tell what I want. I still feel
childishly that the world owes me
kindness and a mother is a collector
of both clutter and debt. And
daughters—the way their hearts break,
there's no poem in it, just the wind
screaming *kiss me kiss me kiss me kiss me love me*
*love me love me love me*

# THE OTHER EARRING

A few of your friends rowed out at night wanting
to find treasure even though the sea was black, because
it was the American way. Combing the tide
on foot I found a constellation
of rings half-buried in sand that must
have washed up from some commercial
wreck. Watery reflections studded
the black sky with gold-plated stars—
snakes and stones and sacred hearts
and a sapphire pierced with a golden hoop.
Jeans soaked, you found the other
earring. When I pointed it out
you pushed the hinge through
the flesh of your ear. Pomegranate bled
from the lobe; I changed my own
earring to wear the matching prize.
A philosophy of my mother's
church attributes the want
to wear earrings from the sea to God.
That's the problem with me—
I never know if I really want something
or if it's God wanting through me.
Now every time I see someone pretty

I just want to kiss you. Now
my body wants to spill out of its skin and wet
everyone like the first dozen rows of an aquatic show.
And after every now comes the next, always and          .
always and always. God never knows what it wants until I want. God
I want to want. God I want to be
wanted. A terrible want—I'm terrible
at being wanted and at wanting too. Maybe someday
I'll want the world. Sorry, I'm preaching
the gospel of the God in the explanation.
I'm wearing the God in the earring.

## FIRE ESCAPE

*It would've been humid*
*when you walked home.*

*Counted your tips.*
*Spent them on groceries*
*not frivolities.*

*Did a sheet mask. Had a cold pudding.*
*Realized you weren't disposable.*

*Forgot the morning's*
*grievances. What the movies get right:*
*the indifference of toll workers,*

*almost godlike. Take the smoke*
*in half gasps to prolong it.*

*Sit for a few hours*
*to the waterfall*
*of beer and ovation*

*from the pub across the road*
*in a white t-shirt*

*from an old lover*
*until the fog*
*of coffee and cooking grease*

*slinks up from*
*the kitchen downstairs.*

# IN YET ANOTHER

i trip over
the same stair over
and over and over
prometheus of just
the one second
the one stair

# SONG OF THE BOWSTRING

Do you know how hard
it is to be too old for anger
and too young to know kindness
is on the horizon? Yeah,
yeah, you do. Sorry I asked.
Sometimes I feel so alone
in my suffering. Sometimes
I'm one birthday candle short.
Sometimes I'm the spent wick.

# I LOVE YOU. I'M SORRY.

If rabbits don't have vocal cords, then
what do they do when they're in distress? pain?
I sat down in the middle of the sidewalk to write
to you. Like Billy Collins I bow to solitude
to while away at invented instruments.
Practice serenades. I'm used to the plane-crash
strings, the drowning brass, even the marimba
managing to flutter so violently my brain suffers
an influx of death a thousand different ways.
Google tells me a frequently asked question is *why do*
*rabbits scream* but fun fact they don't.
Then I open the bedroom door and no one has witnessed it and
a rabbit scream is in fact all the air "being forced out of its lungs all of a sudden."
I want to tell you about the time I fell off an August ferry
in a cloud of mid-afternoon smoke and tears. I've stood waiting,
rain falling in a parabola above me, for a bus
that didn't come because it didn't love me back.
At least according to Google. You'd understand.
I stepped into a museum for shelter
and made eye contact with a statue.
It jerked off the pedestal and broke like an egg
on the kitchen floor. Before I went to sleep I
left a lipstick mark on a light switch.
All I could do was think of you.

# YELLOW LIGHT

That summer the knife slid so sweetly
into the navel orange on the chopping board

and our lips were so sticky
we kissed and they bled.

Magpie-minded since childhood, we hung
a sprig of rosemary in a bottle-shard window

and I made you come on the kitchen counter,
the cabinet door hanging off its hinge.

Your thighs smelled like
citrus for weeks. Your voice

sounds deeper in my memory
but has always been enough to turn

my teeth to stones that you gamble
and I spend. We heimliched the fireplace

till we were black and blue.
Aretha spinning hymns in the den

on a broken dinner plate.
The bedroom, we didn't touch

until it got so cold we finally paid
for heating.

# IV. THE OCEAN

Through the wood's foliage the blue canvas of a roof
looked like an ocean to long for. You tell me
every day that I led you to its shore, held your hand
and touched it to the tide. Don't you remember how you
were the one who parted the ferns and saw wine? And
the slice of moon rose over our heads and I named it
water. I painted you the ships slivering salt
in the skyline but you called them ours and showed me smoke
as it bloated the hurricane above the water, and all of a
sudden we were seafarers. Howling at the moon.
But we never invented any islands, no cove with a tavern.
The night an infinite bruise we tendered and rode.
I could give you a telescope or a book, even a city.
For now, you're content with us cavorting like pirates
but soon you'll hit your shovel against the day
so high you can't see the horizon, and with it, me...

# LIFE AFTER ME

I want to be as honest as selenite and the bands
of light that move through it. Like halos of cherubs
tattooed on men who fall for girls and their kindness.
Be not afraid of wanting. Holding up a lobe of lung
in each hand, squeezed tighter than diamonds
at the approach of the highway tunnel, void
skewering midday, as if it suddenly became the sideways
surface of a moonlit hotel pool I descended into
with my mother. And the first glimpse of day
is always a relief then the promise of light grows
unbearable and can I make it to the end?
Touch the bottom and flutter back to surface without
opening my lungs to moving shadow? I haven't
gone swimming in years and the moonlight's sinking
and when my lungs release it's not water
that rushes in but knowledge:

                              There will be life after me.
You'll move on. There will come a time when they talk
about me the way they talk about their exes. The trusting
smile she aims at me now will look naive in hindsight.
They'll be praying for me in basements across the West,
those animals who don't know they're animal
till there are mice between their teeth. Love gave me

what I didn't ask for but beauty keeps my face pressed
to moonlight, burns harder than breath, is the closest
I'll come to composing a symphony and in the end
we can only do the work of believing for ourselves.
This is the life I should have been leading. All along.

# WILD HEART

Machines breathed night into your heart below
the hospital bed through time and fire to
the other side of the globe yesterday
where my body flew out of bed and in
its pale gown swayed gently down empty streets
winding between sleeping cars and over
iridescent asphalt beneath streetlights
into a barren arena strewn with
what the cleaning crew neglected to sweep
up before they clocked out hours ago:
confetti of popcorn tissue paper
and rose petals, my hands in revelry
reaching for silver dollars and strands of
pretty hair, the day opening above
the catwalks, and the cigarette I lit

# REMEDIAL QUANTUM THEORY
*after Franny Choi*

Out the window,
infinite more universe
than all humanity can
map ashore of dreaming—
the only small instinct
is to expand.
Even the doormat, wilted,
did not turn away what the sole
unburdened. Will some lie cradled
in a planet's skin, shimmying up
tall-willed things
                         craning necks if
they have necks to crane to will to look?
Will they wonder
if they are alone and if they are not
then
      offer their very best wishes and
if a wish will be whispered will it be
swallowed as a kiss by the molecule-thin
shroud their blood sings to?
Can sparks of snow in a metal
cathedral will one universe that matters if

no one breathed a bacterial life?
Life less soft than it is surefire
liquid in green primordial curry—
mass which only a mother
could separate from death.
The moon sounds like a piano
played underwater. Antinomy
will search for names
in some softness that wills no name.
Survivorship takes no names
but the privilege of antinomy.
Look upon
the mountains and

                    gently weep.

# LOVE, HONOUR, & OTHER STORIES

*Dollar bills rescued*
*from the laundry, numbers kissed*
*onto napkins, books*
*bloating in water, photos*
*and getaway cars, hand-poked*
*and gone.*

# IN ANOTHER THE SKY

began to darken
over father and toddling
daughter rounding into a loop
where red buses stood
which could have been
not red but a reflection
of the sky's pulsing flank
one last passenger's heel
snatching in through closing
doors as each bus pulled away
and left the lot until only a few
driverless ones remained
sitting in winter air like clouds
on the bloody under-
belly of the horizon

when i woke i knew to call
but by then you were gone
red and blue gathering
on the sky's lip the quiet
rumble of a bruise

## V. WINTER

Snow                    from            his  mouth
              drifts
  brilliant                              as
opal
              onto      my
                        eyelashes.
                                      We          count
        four      young
        flower    heads.
Spring                  in    my            body
                                                enters
      and    exits
              a      circle    of      crocus    chambers,
              the      bulbs
    you      planted                months      ago
 on    a      golden    hill    running  wet
              with      my
                        blood.

## VI. SPRING

Violet blush, steamed rice earth, grass bent
to the weight of the sky's gentle
burden. You've sipped this song before:
*Rise up, my love, let juniper*
*woo you from the fog.*
We're soaked and we've stolen his gin.

# VII. THE RIDE

There's a city suspended in every second
Such as the one where the first droplet of wine
Rubs your throat and your eyes
Flicker shut.

And I'm content to have these cities to ourselves
Bustling as they are with schools
And apothecaries, little cafes which
Serve wine and whiskey.

Open a newspaper, tilt your head back,
Let sunlight guide your daydream eyes
Over lavender fields
Hurtling past.

# APRÈS

I had a dream; we misbehaved together.

You ran one yellow light and the next, a whole row of them.

I cling to beauty and privilege the way maples do, the way my parents did.

Again and again I've abandoned my urgency

for the romance of cruelty.

# FRONT DESK

They wake,
bring their most

intimate requests, their most
obscure complaints
and offhand confessions.

Dust swept from the crevices,
moon beaten off the bedspread, faces

untranslated and untucked.
Pay the tab, turn in the key.

A food delivery worker waits
texting in neon epaulettes

to take the new housekeeper to bed.
Help her forget
the disaster of the shift.

Everywhere the tech
of desire moves, whirs
beneath economy.

*We compare methodologies,*
*keep each other near.*

# THE RETURNING

*after C Pam Zhang's* How Much of These Hills Is Gold

Wind wails in the body, scalp flapping open to the sky.

Domesticity was invented to scatter the home

That keeps this spirit settled.

Like a beetle finding warmth in dead pine,

Smelling precious fungus across

      The ocean of its distribution,

Did dignity never occur to rotting wood?

It whispers across railway tracks,

Combs boughs and sets fires to

Land untouched by foot.

Only hands were needed,

The rest pilfered for firewood,

Quartered femur, tied with string

and little resistance.

Campfire

Water boiling over tin

Embers

Dirt floating in piss

Black ash bootprint

One orange spark swimming for the night,

Too red to be a star, reckless,

Fire's offspring never looking back at the chasm,

Zigzagging for a piece of heaven settled between

Silver dollars flashing in the sky

Because the next place might be better.

# EROS

When my father held me up to a mirror
        as a babe I thought I knew

what object permanence was, knew

what turned the mess between my legs into
        the sour purple knot
you'd find at the bottom of a day-old wine glass.

Every time I saw you
        it was like the last time.
Like the meteor shower at the end of the earth

you know you won't forget for the rest of your life

because the rest of your life will last only seconds.
        If spoken, it's gospel.

No need to measure what's inside your head
with an other.

It's all the same, baby, damn.

# SEPTEMBER

It started raining when my high kicked in.
That's fall for you: a paranoia
that you can get caught stealing pleasure.
A woman danced in front of the window
for a few seconds before walking on,
oblivious to me behind the blinds. I'm sick
of outsourcing care to desire.
Knead the muscles along my spine; clean up
after my disgust. Touch me how
morning light faints across a mountainside
and its velvet trees, ladylike.
Where I am now, the cracked window
admits the smell of sea, that oyster tang
and saline sunshine. My home hangs on the lip
of a cliff. There's a small writing desk
my co-worker was getting rid of; toiletries include
an ashtray by the sink. Jewellery from you
sits in vintage boxes beside my desk.
What would I have known of life on the coast
—the water the cats the diners the trains
the sunsets and this sweetness—
if not for evangelicalism?
I had visions of wearing the gifts

you gave me moments before
our tectonic demise. Champagne Swarovski
crystals, exacting in their shine, a rope
of starlight to ensnare the wrist.
The world once divided neatly
into shadow and light. My flight
from knowledge of good and evil was more
a flight from belief that you can do something
right, take away the pain, written into moral
imaginaries of the retina. We wear our bright
flurries of thought. Fry bacon with windows
open to the chill. It took me
a while to realize every bad thing
I did went unpunished. I'm brought
back to hot herbal tea and bike rides
down to the river with stinging hands.
My sibling and mother wait at home.

# COMMISSION:

A statue of my exact form touchable like a soapstone lover like the touch of a hand on a woman's waist or is it a woman's hand round a scotch neat or the clouds rolling over the edge of the clock (or over the edge of a skirt?) or my lips on the doorstep of home or a storm jilting a jet in the sky or the rain taking our hair in its mouth or dust dressing a dog-eared book or a cufflink wandering behind the bedside table or how the piano coos on a snowy day as if it could kiss like aftershave because music never sounds so alive as it does played after the performance is over

# TSURUNE

*Golden shovel after Ocean Vuong*

The pain demands I
look up to a scene of might
and beauty. I've still

loved in rain, to be
honest, its scent and veil too.
I felt almost young

to survive—let in
my hunger and let in my
rage, humming with grief.

Two lives trying to
make up for the other, know
when to defer, where

to rear back for it.
To determine how it ends.

# SACRED HEART

or maybe a heart's
a mystery novel:
>                    red as velvet, smell of exhaust,
>                    neon vacancy sign sputtering messages addressed
>                    to you when your back's turned. all the alleged complexity
of humanity in its pores, striated
for consumption by chemical processes.

the convergence of lives, motivations
>                    riding shotgun with oxygen through walls
>                    like ghosts, cycled through social
>                    worlds in roulette chambers.
windows turning away, windows shading their eyes. everything

hapless to the rhythm, the elevator grace,
each pulse bringing that blaze of
>                    iron and jazz,
in communion producing something
quantifiably and qualitatively more magic
>                    than flesh and air.

# NOTES & ACKNOWLEDGEMENTS

Previous versions of these poems first appeared in *Pinhole Poetry* ("Glue Trap," "Clover"), *Canthius* ("Lucky Strike," "Rationale"), *Contemporary Verse 2* ("Heat Wave"), *Four Way Review* ("When Billie Holiday Sang"), *Plainsongs* ("Intermission"), *petrichor* ("September"), *filling Station* ("Sacred Heart"), and my chapbook from Bottlecap Press, *We Search For God on Mars* ("Exodus," "The Returning," "Remedial Quantum Theory"). "Clover" was also published in *Pinhole Poetry Volume One Selected* chapbook.

"When Billie Holiday Sang" quotes her song "Come Rain or Come Shine."

"I Love You. I'm Sorry" references the closing lines of Billy Collins's poem "Serenade": "...looking down at me as I finger / a nameless instrument / it took so many days and nights to invent."

The title "My Year of Rest & Expatriation" plays on Ottessa Moshfegh's *My Year of Rest and Relaxation,* and the Phoebe Bridgers song referenced is "ICU."

"Wild Heart" is titled after the Bleachers song.

Franny Choi's *Soft Science* inspired "Remedial Quantum Theory."

The phrase "tech of desire" in "Front Desk" comes from Rhiannon McGavin's poem "Luddite Habits."

"The Returning" was constructed around lines from C Pam Zhang's novel *How Much of These Hills Is Gold*: "Home keeps the spirits settled" and "The next place might be better."

"September" was drafted in a Kundiman workshop ("Writing Letters to Ghosts") led by Jennifer S. Chen.

"Tsurune" is a golden shovel written after a quote from an interview with Ocean Vuong: "I might still be too young in my grief to know where it ends."

Heather O'Neill's *The Lonely Hearts Hotel* influenced the title of the book and is one of my favourite novels.

Cherie, thank you for being the first reader of some of the most urgent poems here. Grace Epstein, thank you always for your friendship, for the intellect of your feedback, for hate-watching *The Bachelor* with me, among other things. This collection of poems wouldn't have emerged if it weren't for our poetry exchanges and workshopping sessions.

Photo by Lydia Taylor

**GRACE KWAN** is a Malaysian-born sociologist and writer based in "Vancouver," the unceded territories of the Musqueam, Squamish, and Tsleil-Waututh peoples. Their recent poetry appears in *Canthius, Room Magazine,* and others. Find them at grckwn.com.

# MORE FROM METONYMY PRESS

*El Ghourabaa: A Queer and Trans Collection of Oddities*
edited by Eli Tareq El Bechelany-Lynch and Samia Marshy

*The Haunting of Adrian Yates* by Markus Harwood-Jones

*The Rage Letters* by Valérie Bah, translated by Kama La Mackerel

*LOTE* by Shola von Reinhold

*The Good Arabs* by Eli Tareq El Bechelany-Lynch

*Personal Attention Roleplay* by H Felix Chau Bradley

*A Natural History of Transition* by Callum Angus

*Dear Black Girls* by Shanice Nicole and Kezna Dalz

*ZOM-FAM* by Kama La Mackerel

*Dear Twin* by Addie Tsai

*Little Blue Encyclopedia (for Vivian)* by Hazel Jane Plante

*nîtisânak* by Jas M. Morgan

*Lyric Sexology Vol. 1* by Trish Salah

*Fierce Femmes and Notorious Liars:*
*A Dangerous Trans Girl's Confabulous Memoir* by Kai Cheng Thom

*Small Beauty* by jiaqing wilson-yang

*She Is Sitting in the Night: Re-visioning Thea's Tarot*
by Oliver Pickle and Ruth West